THE PSALTER
OF AVRAM HAKTANI

Also by A. M. KLEIN

HATH NOT A JEW................Behrman's, N. Y.

THE HITLERIAD.............New Directions, N. Y.

POEMS

by

A. M. KLEIN

PHILADELPHIA

THE JEWISH PUBLICATION SOCIETY OF AMERICA

5705–1944

DEDICATED TO

The Memory of My Father

ACKNOWLEDGEMENTS

Thanks are due to the editors of the following periodicals for permission to reprint poems that appeared in their pages: *Poetry: A Magazine of Verse; The Menorah Journal; New Directions Annual; Opinion: A Magazine of Jewish Life and Letters; The Canadian Forum; The Reconstructionist; First Statement;* and *Preview.*

CONTENTS

THE PSALTER
OF AVRAM HAKTANI

PSALM I

A psalm of Abraham, when he hearkened to
a voice, and there was none:

SINCE prophecy has vanished out of Israel,
And since the open vision is no more,
Neither a word on the high places, nor the Urim
    and Thummim,
Nor even a witch, foretelling, at En-dor, —
Where in these dubious days shall I take counsel?
Who is there to resolve the dark, the doubt?

    O, these are the days of scorpions and of whips
    When all the seers have had their eyes put out,
    And all the prophets burned upon the lips!

There is noise only in the groves of Baal.
Only the painted heathen dance and sing,
With frenzied clamouring.
Among the holy ones, however, is no sound at all.

PSALM II

*Maschil of Abraham: A prayer when
he was in the cave:*

HOW is he changed, the scoffers say,
This hero of an earlier day,
Who in his youth did battle with
The wicked theologic myth;
Who daily from his pocket drew
(*Aetat.* sixteen) a writing, true,
Attested, sealed, and signed, its gist:
God swearing He did not exist;
Who in his Zion lay at ease
Concocting learned blasphemies
To hate, contemn, and ridicule
The godly reign, the godly rule.
How is he now become as one
Trembling with age before the Throne,—
This XXth century scientist,
A writer of psalms, a liturgist;
A babbling pious woman, he
Who boasted that his thoughts were free,
And who at worst did nullify
By ignorance the deity.

O Lord, in this my thirtieth year
What clever answer shall I bear

To those slick persons amongst whom
I sat, but was not in their room?
How shall I make apocalypse
Of that which rises to my lips,
And on my lips is smitten dumb: —
Elusive word, forgotten sum.

O could I for a moment spare
My eyes to them, or let them hear
The music that about me sings,
Then might they cease their twitterings.

Then might they also know, as I,
The undebatable verity,
The truth unsoiled by epigram,
The simple *I am that I am*.
But failing these powers in me, Lord,
Do Thou the deed, say Thou the word,
And with Thy sacred stratagem
Do justify my ways to them.

PSALM III

A Psalm of Abraham, when he was sore pressed:

WOULD that the Lord had made me, in place
    of man-child, beast!
Even an ox of the field, content on grass,
On clover and cud content, had made me, made me
    the least
Of his creatures, one of a herd, to pass
As cattle, pastured and driven and sold and bought
To toil on ploughland or before a cart!
For easier is the yoke than the weight of thought,
Lighter the harness than the harnessed heart!

4

PSALM IV

A psalm of Abraham, touching
his green pastures:

FROM pastures green, whereon I lie,
Beside still waters, far from crowds,
I lift hosannahs to the sky
And hallelujahs to the clouds,

Only to see where clouds should sit,
And in that space the sky should fill,
The fierce carnivorous Messerschmidt,
The Heinkel on the kill.

They'll not be green for very long,
Those pastures of my peace, nor will
The heavens be a place for song,
Nor the still waters still.

PSALM V

A song of degrees:

CONSIDER the son of man, how he doth get him knowledge
and wisdom!

Not to the sorcerer does he go, nor yet to the maker of books;
not from the gait of angels does he take example; he
mimics not the antics of the cherubim.

The beasts of the field are his teachers; feather and fur his
instructors, instructing him the way that he shall go
therein.

Before their hooves, he sits, a disciple; to the eyrie, he climbs,
crying, *Master, Master.*

To the ape he bows down, the ape, flinging the cocoafruit,
devising slings.

He worships the elephant for that he has an ivory sword.

He sees the bow of the porcupine, and the arrows of his quills;
a parable in shell the tortoise brings to him.

Even the noisome beast, whose spikenard sendeth forth the
smell thereof, instructs him how that the enemy may be
abashed.

How wonderful, therefore, is this son of man, who lets no
pride between him and his doctors, —

Yea, at this very instant, he gapes at the eagle's talons drop-
ping volcanic rock.

6

PSALM VI

A psalm of Abraham, concerning that which
he beheld upon the heavenly scarp:

I

AND on that day, upon the heavenly scarp,
The hosannahs ceased, the hallelujahs died,
And music trembled on the silenced harp.
An angel, doffing his seraphic pride,
Wept; and his tears so bitter were, and sharp,
That where they fell, the blossoms shrivelled
    and died.

II

Another with such voice intoned the psalm
It sang forth blasphemy against the Lord.
Oh, that was a very imp in angeldom
Who, thinking evil, said no evil word —
But only pointed, at each *Te Deum*
Down to the earth, and its unspeakable horde.

III

The Lord looked down, and saw the cattle-cars:
Men ululating to a frozen land.
He saw a man tear at his flogged scars,
And saw a babe look for its blown-off hand.
Scholars, he saw, sniffing their bottled wars,
And doctors who had geniuses unmanned.

IV

The gentle violinist whose fingers played
Such godly music, washing a pavement, with
    lye,
He saw. He heard the priest who called His aid.
He heard the agnostic's undirected cry.
Unto Him came the odor Hunger made,
And the odor of blood before it is quite dry.

V

The angel who wept looked into the eyes of God.
The angel who sang ceased pointing to the earth.
A little cherub who'd spied the earthly sod
Went mad, and flapped his wings in crazy mirth.
And the good Lord said nothing, but with a nod
Summoned the angels of Sodom down to earth.

PSALM VII

For the chief physician:

A song for hunters: In that wood,
That whispering jungle of the blood
Where the carnivorous midge seeks meat,
And yawns the sinuous spirochete,
And roars the small fierce unicorn,
The white-robed hunters sound the horn.
May they have goodly hunting. May
Their quarry soon be brought to bay.

PSALM VIII

Psalm of the fruitful field:

A FIELD in sunshine is a field
On which God's signature is sealed;
When clouds above the meadows go,
The heart knows peace; the birds fly low.
O field at dusk! O field at dawn!
O golden hay in the golden sun!
O field of golden fireflies
Bringing to earth the starry skies!
You touch the mind with many a gem;
Dewdrops upon the sun's laced hem;
Young dandelions with coronets;
Old ones with beards; pale violets
Sleeping on moss, like princesses;
Sweet clover, purple, odorous;
Fat bees that drowse themselves to sleep
In honey-pots that daisies keep;
Birds in the hedge; and in the ditch
Strawberries growing plump and rich.
Who clamors for a witch's brew
Potioned from hellebore and rue;
Or pagan imps of fairy band,
When merely field and meadowland
Can teach a lad that there are things
That set upon his shoulders wings?

Even a cow that lolls it's tongue
Over a buttercup, swells song
In any but a devil's lung.
Even a sheep which rolls in grass
Is happier than lad or lass,
Who treads on stones in streets of brass.
Who does not love a field lacks wit,
And he were better under it!
And as for me let paradise
Set me in fields with sunny skies.
And grant my soul in after days
In clovered meadowlands to graze.

PSALM IX

A psalm, to be preserved against
two wicked words:

I AM not of the saints, O Lord, to wear
The broken shoes of poverty, and dance.
For I am made sick at heart with terrible fear
Seeing the poor man spurned, looked at askance,
Standing, his cap in hand, and speaking low,
And never getting his fellow's heart or ear.
O may I never beg my daily bread,
Never efface my pride, like a dirty word;
And never grovel that my little chick be fed.
Preserve me from poverty, O Lord.

Preserve me, too, and Thou who knowest hearts,
Know'st this prayer does from the heart arise,
Preserve me from possessions, from the marts,
The mints, the mansions, all the worldly goods,
Debasing even the man of noblest parts.

From too much wealth that warps the very saints,
From power that ambushes the soul by stealth,
From suzerainty that fevers, and then faints:
Preserve me, Lord, from wealth.

But in Thy wisdom Thou canst so ordain
That wealth and poverty be known no more.
Then hadst Thou answered me, again and again,
Answered Thy servant, neither rich nor poor.

PSALM X

Lamed Vav: A psalm to utter in memory
of great goodness:

Under a humble name he came to us;
Died; and left his wife executrix
Of tears, and a name for which the saints
    would fuss. —
I believe that he was one of the Thirty-six . . .

PSALM XI

A psalm of a mighty hunter before the Lord:

O, NOT for furs,
And not for feathers,
Did Chatzkel the hunter
Weather all weathers!

Neither the crow,
Nor the shy sparrow
Had fear of his bow
And rotted arrow.

A hunter he was,
Who bore no rifle
Whose snare did not kill,
Nor lariat stifle.

A dearth in the land:
Beasts die of famine —
Chatzkel the hunter
Leaves his backgammon

Traps him some wild beasts,
Keeps them in cages,
Until the hot sun will
Have spent its rages.

15

Meanwhile the tiger
Eats tiger-lilies,
And milk is fed to
The wild colt's fillies.

Upon his wrist-bone
The robin settles;
While Chatzkel crams her
With lilac petals.

And then, in the Spring-time
Chatzkel sets free
Beast and bird under
The greenwood tree.

O, what was Nimrod
Who used strength, not skill,
To quell the forest,
Compared to Chatzkel,

Chatzkel who whistled
To catch a bird;
Who hallooed, and found him
In midst of a herd?

PSALM XII

To the chief musician, who played
for the dancers:

THESE were the ones who thanked their **God**
With dancing jubilant shins:
The beggar, who for figleaf pride
Sold shoelaces and pins;
The blindman for his brotherly dog;
The cripple for his chair;
The mauled one for the blessed gasp
Of the cone of sweet kind air.
I did not see this dance, but men
Have praised its grace; yet I
Still cannot fathom how they danced,
Or why.

PSALM XIII

A song for wanderers:

WHAT was the song the gypsy sang
Singing to his fiddle?
The open road, and the pleasant place,
The sun that shines with a gypsy face,
The two halves of the beautiful world,
And O, himself in the middle!

What was the song the sailor sang
To the wind's soughing?
The silver on the moonlit sea,
The stars for jolly company,
The harbor pub, and the girl in port,
And O, a good wind blowing!

What was the song the weary Jew
Sang to his sorrow?
No song at all made sweet his lips,
Not of travelled roads nor travelling ships.
No song today wells from the heart
That has no morrow!

PSALM XIV

A psalm for five holy pilgrims, yea, six
on the King's highway:

ONE comes: — he is a very blossoming tree —
With frankincense and perfumery:
Sweet savour for his nostril'd deity.

Another bears God trinkets, smooth and rich,
And little idols polished overmuch —
All holy objects pleasant to the touch.

And still another seeks the mystic word
With all the rainbows of his jewelled hoard —
His goodly proffer to the sight of the Lord.

With delicates and sweetmeats and with fruit,
Food of the blossom, eating of the root,
Comes one to flatter the taste of the Absolute.

And the fifth pilgrim trips upon the sod,
Blowing sweet music from a hollow rod:
Sounds gratifying to the ear of God.

Not sight, sound, smell, taste, touch, his freight,
One brings his heart for pawning with his fate:
He, surely, he shall come within the Gate!

PSALM XV

*A psalm of Abraham, touching the crown with which
he was crowned on the day of his espousals:*

THIS is the man who brought to me
The thumb-print of the Deity;
Who hung upon my hairless chest
The fringed talismanic vest;
This is the Jew who once did hem
My heart with old Jerusalem;
Who solved each letter's mystic hook
Upon the parchment Pentateuch,
And poured me out the *kiddush*-wine,
Sparkling with all the clandestine
Eye-winks of angels; this is he
Who made my youth worth memory.
Most fitting is it, then, that this
Old Rabbi, Eden-bent, should now
Sanctify our marriage-vow.

PSALM XVI

*To the chief scribe, a psalm of Abraham, in the
day of the gladness of his heart:*

PREPARE the inks, the red, the green, the black;
Thicken the paints, the purple and the gold;
Make smooth the goatskin; fatten each wry crack;
Wash out the clotted brush, and shape some old
And many-flourished symbol in its track.

Take hold your quill, meticulously cleanse
Its point, and thinly trace the guiding line;
Affix to your left eye the perfect lens,
Then write in the square letter, black and fine,
To wit: *That love will never wander hence.*

And unto this last final verse,
Add my name, and add hers.

PSALM XVII

For the bridegroom coming out of his
chamber, a song:

THE young men with the sparse beards laud
    the bride;
"She puts no rouges to her lips; no small
Black beauty spots upon her cheeks; no pall
Of perfumed dust upon her neck; no dyed
Resplendence on her lovely head; no pride
Of henna on her finger-nails at all;
Yet is she very beautiful withal,
Most beautiful and yet not beautified."
The long-haired virgins musically doff
Their silence, and around the bridegroom wheel,
Singing his bride and all the seven days' love
That will be hers anon, the nuptial weal
That he will serve; in evidence whereof
He breaks the wineglass underneath his heel.

PSALM XVIII

For the bride, a song, to be sung by virgins:

SHE has laved her body in living water. She
    Has touched no food all day. She is most pale.
Her face is white. That she lives one can see
    Only by the quivering of her veil.

The vile tongue falters; it can bear no tale.
    Speak of the dove, if you will speak of her.
She is a flower. She is flower-frail.
    Regard her. She is virgin. She is pure.

PSALM XIX

A benediction:

O BRIDEGROOM eager for the bride,
O white-veiled bride,
May love be on your pillow; may
    The quiet turtledove preside
Your sweet consortments night and day;
May the months be fat for you; bask
    In the sun; love in the moon; let bread
    Be never wanting from your table,
        Wine from your cask,
        Warmth from your bed.
O let the almond flourish on your tree,
O let the grape grow big, and full of juice
    And of the perfect shape:
Let nine months grow diffuse, and wax and grow diffuse,
    And let the first-born be.

PSALM XX

A psalm of Abraham, which he
made at the feast:

BRING on the rich, the golden-dotted soup;
Set down the viands, odorous of spice;
Let the plate steam with capons; fetch the pies;
Add tender chicken to this fragrant group.

Forget not, prithee, the replenished fish
Smacking of sea and land and heaven; fill
Each plate to a most toothsome pinnacle;
Make a small Lebanon of every dish.

The pickled tongue must find its place; the roast,
Sending enticements to the nostrils, must
Show promise of soft meat and tasty crust; —
O cooks, belittle not the bridegroom-host!

Unseal the bottles of grandfather's day;
And empty them into the goblets; then
Empty the goblets to be filled again;
Let wine say what dry tongues can never say.

When clean bones and dry flasks will be the trace,
The only trace that here has been a feast,
Then let each voice find its own strength increased
To laud the Lord with a well-chanted grace!

25

PSALM XXI

A benediction for the new moon:

ELDER, behold the Shunamite, the rumor of
  her face,
And young man, know, the mirror of thy love!

Praise ye, therefore, the moon: each after his
  own fashion!
Sing ye a song:
The warrior for the brass buckler of David;
The learned man in his tent
For the bright candle smiling on his book.
Before that newly-minted coin
Rub, O little merchantman, thy joyous palms!

For the weaver of your tides,
Sing, O mariners, shuttlers of ships!
Praise it, O hunters, the hind you cannot stalk!

Lift up your heels; lift up your eyes to see,
Each after his own fashion, the seal of God
Impressed upon His open writ!

26

PSALM XXII

A prayer of Abraham, against madness:

LORD, for the days allotted me,
Preserve me whole, preserve me hale!
Spare me the scourge of surgery.
Let not my blood nor members fail.

But if Thy will is otherwise,
And I am chosen such an one
For maiming and for maladies -
So be it; and Thy will be done.

Palsy the keepers of the house;
And of the strongmen take Thy toll.
Break down the twigs; break down
    the boughs.
But touch not, Lord, the golden bowl!

O, I have seen these touched ones —
Their fallow looks, their barren eyes —
For whom have perished all the suns
And vanished all fertilities;

Who, docile, sit within their cells
Like weeds, within a stagnant pool.

I have seen also their fierce hells,
Their flight from echo, their fight
     with ghoul.

Behold him scrabbling on the door!
His spittle falls upon his beard,
As, cowering, he whines before
The voices and the visions, feared.

Not these can serve Thee. Lord,
     if such
The stumbling that awaits my path —
Grant me Thy grace, thy mortal
     touch,
The full death-quiver of Thy wrath!

PSALM XXIII

A psalm of justice, and its scales:

ONE day the signal shall be given me;
I shall break in and enter heaven, and,
Remembering who, below, held upper hand,
And who was trodden into misery, —
I shall seek out the abominable scales
On which the heavenly justice is mis-weighed.
I know I am no master of the trade,
Can neither mend nor make, clumsy with nails,
No artisan, — yet am I so forespoken,
Determined so against the automaton,
That I must tamper with it, tree and token,
Break bolts, undo its markings, one by one,
And leave those scales so gloriously broken,
That ever thereafter justice shall be done!

PSALM XXIV

Shiggaion of Abraham which he
sang unto the Lord:

O INCOGNITO god, anonymous lord,
with what name shall I call you? Where shall I
discover the syllable, the mystic word
that shall evoke you from eternity?
Is that sweet sound a heart makes, clocking life,
Your appellation? Is the noise of thunder, it?
Is it the hush of peace, the sound of strife?

I have no title for your glorious throne,
and for your presence not a golden word, —
only that wanting you, by that alone
I do evoke you, knowing I am heard.

PSALM XXV

To the prophets, minor and major,
a Psalm or Song:

THEY are upon us, the prophets, minor and major!
Madame Yolanda rubs the foggy crystal.
She peers, she ponders, the future does engage her;
She sees the *Fuehrer* purged by Nazi pistol.

Sir Aries Virgo, astrology-professor,
Regards the stars, and prophesies five truces.
Herr Otto Shprinzen, of the same guild, a guesser,
From the same stars the contrary deduces.

They too have thoughts, those scriptural inspectors;
They count the verses, the hapaxlegomena,
By means of esoterical detectors
Foretell next year's right-guaranteed phenomena.

Ides is foretold, and doomsday, and God's thunders.
January greets the unseen with a seer.
Augurs prognosticate, from signs and wonders,
Many a cradle, yea, and many a bier.

These, then, the soothsayers, and this their season:
But where, O where is that inspired peasant,
That prophet, not of the remote occasion,
But who will explicate the folded present?

31

PSALM XXVI

To the chief Musician, a Psalm of Israel,
to bring to remembrance:

BY THE rivers of Babylon, there we sat down, we wept
When we remembered Zion, —
O they are many that have had our tears!
The alluvium of Nilus is still fat
With the tender little bones of our firstborn,
And Tiber is still yellow like our badge.
Shall one forget the bears, and the Jews like bears
That danced on the shores of the savage Vistula?
Forget the crystal streams of castled Spain
So many fires failed to boil to salt?
Forget the Rhine? O Rhenish wines are sharp.
The subtle salt of blood gives them their sharpness.

Gatner them up, O Lord, these many rivers,
And dry them in the furnace of Thy wrath!
Let them not be remembered! Let them be
So many soon-to-be forgotten clouds
Dropping their rain
Upon the waters of Thy favorite Jordan!

PSALM XXVII

A psalm to teach humility:

O SIGN and wonder of the barnyard, more
beautiful than the pheasant, more melodious
than nightingale! O creature marvellous!

Prophet of sunrise, and foreteller of times!
Vizier of the constellations! Sage,
red-bearded, scarlet-turbaned, in whose brain
the stars lie scattered like well-scattered grain!

Calligraphist upon the barnyard page!
Five-noted balladist! Crower of rhymes!

O morning-glory mouth, O throat of dew,
announcing the out-faring of the blue,
the greying and the going of the night,
the coming on,
the imminent coming of the dawn,
the coming of the kinsman, the brightly-plumaged sun!

O creature marvellous — and O blessed Creator,
Who givest to the rooster wit
to know the movements of the turning day,
to understand, to herald it,
better than I, who neither sing nor crow
and of the sun's goings and comings nothing know.

33

PSALM XXVIII

A psalm or prayer — praying his
portion with beasts:

THE better to understand Thy ways,
Divinity I would divine,
Let me companion all my days
The more-than-human beasts of Thine;

The sheep whose little woolly throat
Taught the child Isaac sacrifice;
The dove returning to Noah's boat,
Sprigless, and with tearful eyes;

The ass instructing Balaam
The discourse of inspired minds;
And David's lost and bleating lamb,
And Solomon's fleet lovely hinds;

Enfold me in their fold, and let
Me learn their mystic parables —
Of food that desert ravens set,
And of the lion's honeyed fells.

Above all, teach me blessedness
Of him, Azazel, that dear goat,
Sent forth into the wilderness
To hallow it with one sad note.

PSALM XXIX

To the chief musician, a Psalm of the
Bratzlaver, a parable:

AN AGED king, his brittle shins in hose,
Spoonfed, dribbling over a purple bib,
Upon a time and at a banquet board
Raised bony palm, and stayed the resined bows,
And hushed the drums, and stilled the cornet's chord.
Then caused to issue from his seventh rib
These toothless words:

　　　　　　　Thane of four graveyard ells,
Soon shall you mark me, vassal of the worm.
The eager belfry waits to cluck its bells;
The royal sexton, palsied and infirm,
Lets rust grow on his spade, moss on my tomb.
Wherefore, my son, my immortality,
Ascend my throne; don crown; let cannon boom!
For though from my high tower in the sky
My rheumy eyes have seen your star and doom,
Be of good cheer, of noble temper be;
And never let a baneful wind blow dust
Between yourself and your felicity . . .

PSALM XXX

To the chief musician, a psalm of the Bratzlaver,
which he wrote down as the stammerer spoke:

At unprehensile Time, all fingers clutch.
Can it be counted on an abacus?
Or weighed on scales, most delicate to the touch?
Or measured with rods? What Mathematicus
Can speak thereof, save as a net on the brain,
A web some much-afflated spider weaves
On which hang chronicles, like drops of rain?
That, and no more, the quarry he retrieves.
But, truly, in what smithy is it forged?
In what alembic brewed? By what bird hatched?
I, but a stammerer, by the spirit urged,
Having approached that Door, found it unlatched,
Say Time is vacuum, save it be compact
Of men's deeds imitating godly act.

PSALM XXXI

*To the chief musician: a Psalm of the
Bratzlaver, touching a good gardener:*

I

IT WAS a green, a many-meadowed county!
Orchards there were, heavy with fruitage; and
Blossom and bud and benison and bounty

Filled with good odor that luxurious land.
Stained with crushed grass, an old and earthy yeoman
Sceptred that green demesne with pruning wand.

II

Suddenly came the chariots of the foeman;
Suddenly vanished that good gardener, —
Ruled in the land, three companies of bowmen.

One company polluted its sweet air,
Another rendered its ripe fruitage bitter;
A third made foul its beauty which was fair.

People of starving sparrows, loud their twitter!
Wherefore I did bespeak a neighboring folk:
Behold your kin devoured by a wolf's litter,

Release their land, unburden them their yoke
Or similar evil may transgress your borders!

III

Now, though they made them ready, as I spoke,
In tippling and in gluttonish disorders
They tarried on their march, until one day
As they descried the invaders' spectral warders,

Their flagons soured, their viands did decay,
And odor and taste did utterly forsake them.
Then in their sore distress, they sought to pray.

O but my ungraped water did so slake them!
My poor dry crust did such rich taste afford!
They ate, they drank, they slept, and none could
      wake them.

IV

Wherefore, alone, I mingled with the horde,
And unknown walked in many public places.
God save me from the ugly words I heard!

And from those gates, beset by wrothful faces
Where Bribery stretched its hand, and turned its head!
And from quick Lust, and his two-score grimaces!

Salute them, now, three companies of dread:
Filth, in its dun array, the clean taste killing;
Embattled Bribery, with stealthy tread

Advancing on the vanquished, all too-willing
To barter visions for a piece of gold;
And legioned Lust, at its foul buckets swilling . . .

V

They did salute them, did my henchmen bold,
With many a sword, and many an eager arrow,
And driven was the foe from wood and wold.

Then did we come upon him, in a narrow
Streetyard, followed by children, and a cur, —
We brought him fruit, high-pilèd in a barrow,
Gift for a king, — for that good gardener.

PSALM XXXII

A song that the ships of Jaffa did sing in the night:

THE ship leaves Jaffa, treasure in its hold:
Figs, coronets of sweetness; sweeter dates;
Citrons, like perfume phials, packed in crates;
Boxed oranges, the scented globes of gold;
Grape clusters, and wine bottles, dusty, old;
Sweet almonds, toothsomest of delicates;
Bleeding golgothas of red pomegranates;
All smooth and fresh, and innocent of mould.
And Torah scrolls penned by some scribe, now dead,
And pray'r-shawls woven in an eastern loom,
And palm-leaves shipped to the Uncomforted,
And candlesticks to light some Sabbath gloom.
And little sacks of holy earth to spread
Under a pious skull in a far tomb . . .

PSALM XXXIII

A psalm, forbidden to Cohanim:

WHO coming from the synagogue
On Sabbath eves to always find
The sacred Sabbath triple sign —
The burnished candle on the cloth,
The white bread still unbroken, and
The beaker full of hallowed wine, —
Now on this Friday evening waits
For no such signs. His voice is stilled.
There is no soft tread at the door.
The bread is baked, unbroken, and
The beaker is not even filled.

The candles flicker on the floor.

PSALM XXXIV

A psalm of Abraham, to be written down and
left on the tomb of Rashi:

Now, in this terrible tumultuous night,
When roars the metal beast, the steel bird screams,
And images of God, for fraud or fright,
Cannot discern what is from that which seems, —
I, in bewilderment, remember you,
Mild pedagogue, who took me, young and raw,
And led me, verse by verse, and clue by clue,
Mounting the spiral splendid staircase of the Law, —
You, Rabbi Solomon bar Isaac, known
Rashi, incomparable exegete,
Who did sustain my body and my bone
With drink talmudic and with biblic meat, —
Simple, and for a child were they, your words,
Bringing into the silent wooded script,
Texts that came twittering, like learned birds,
Describing mightily the nondescript.
Not these can I forget, nor him ignore,
That old archaic Frank expounding lore
From his Hebraic crypt.

Nothing was difficult, O Master, then,
No query but it had an answer, clear, —
But now though I am grown, a man of men,
The books all read, the places seen, the dear
Too personal heart endured all things, there is

42

Much that I cannot grasp, and much that goes amiss,
And much that is a mystery that even the old Gaul,
Nor Onkelus, nor Jonathan, can lucidate at all.

Yours were such days, great rabbi, like these days,
When blood was spilled upon the public ways,
And lives were stifled for the glut of gore,
As they marched on, those murderous four,
Hunger and hate and pestilence and war!
                    Wherefore, O *Parshandatha* of the law,
Unriddle me the chapter of the week,
Show me the wing, the hand, behind the claw,
The human mouth behind the vulture beak;
Reveal, I pray you, do reveal to me
Behind the veil the vital verity;
Show me again, as you did in my youth
Behind the equivocal text the unequivocal truth!

O vintner of Troyes,
Consider the cluster of my time, its form and shape,
And say what wine will issue from this bitter grape!

I wait your answer; in the interim
I do, for you who left no son to read
The prayer before the sacred cherubim,
Intone, as one who is of your male seed,
A *Kaddish*:
                    May it reach eternity
And grace your soul, and even bring some grace
To most unworthy, doubt-divided me.

PSALM XXXV

*A psalm of Abraham, which he made
because of fear in the night:*

THOU settest them about my bed,
The four good angels of the night,
Invisible wings on left and right,
An holy watch at foot and head:

Gabriel, Uriel, Raphael,
And Michael, of the angelic host
Who guard my sleep-entrusted ghost
Until day break, and break the spell.

Until day break, and shadows pass
My bones lie in a sack of flesh,
My blood lies caught in carmined mesh,
And I am wholly trodden grass.

But those the warders of life and limb
Escort my soul to distant shores,
My soul that in its dreaming soars
With seraphim and cherubim,

To lands unrecognized, to shores
Bright with great sunlight, musical
With singing of such scope and skill,
It is too much for human ears.

I see the angel's drinking-cup,
That flower that so scents the air!
The golden domes! The towers there!
My mind could never think them up!

Yet when the shadows flee away,
And fly the four good angels, and
I fare forth, exiled from that land,
Back to my blood, my bone, my day,

Untowered, unflowered, unscented banks,
Back to the lumpy sack of skin,
The head, the torso, and the shin,
I offer up, to Thee, my thanks.

PSALM XXXVI

A Psalm touching genealogy:

Not sole was I born, but entire genesis:
For to the fathers that begat me, this
Body is residence. Corpuscular,
They dwell in my veins, they eavesdrop at my ear,
They circle, as with Torahs, round my skull,
In exit and in entrance all day pull
The latches of my heart, descend, and rise —
And there look generations through my eyes.

A VOICE WAS HEARD IN RAMAH
SINGLE POEMS

IN RE SOLOMON WARSHAWER

ON Wodin's day, sixth of December, thirty-nine,
I, Friedrich Vercingetorix, attached
to the VIIth Eavesdroppers-behind-the-Line,
did cover my beat, when suddenly the crowd I watched
surrounded, in a cobbled lane one can't pass through,
a bearded man, disguised in rags, a Jew.

In the said crowd there were a number of Poles.
Mainly, however, there were Germans there;
blood-brothers of our Reich, true Aryan souls,
breathing at last — in Warsaw — Nordic air.

These were the words the Jew was shouting:
I took them down verbatim:

Whom have I hurt? Against whose silk have I brushed?
On which of your women looked too long?
I tell you I have done no wrong!
Send home your children, lifting hardened dung,
And let your curs be hushed!
For I am beard and breathlessness, and chased enough.
Leave me in peace, and let me go my way.

At this the good folk laughed. The Jew continued to say
he was no thief, he was a man for hire,
worked for his bread, artist or artisan,

49

a scribe, if you wished, a vendor or a buyer,
work of all kinds, and anything at all:
paint a mural, scour a latrine,
indite an ode, repair an old machine,
anything, to repeat,
anything at all,
so that he might eat
and have his straw couch in his abandoned stall.
Asked for his papers, he made a great to-do
of going through the holes in his rags, whence he withdrew
a Hebrew pamphlet and a signet ring,
herewith produced, Exhibits 1 and 2.

I said: No documents in a civilized tongue?
He replied:

Produce, O Lord, my wretched fingerprint,
Bring forth, O angel in the heavenly court,
My dossier, full, detailed, both fact and hint,
Felony, misdemeanor, tort!

I refused to be impressed by talk of that sort.

From further cross-examination, it appeared,
immediate history: a beggar in Berlin,
chased as a vagrant from the streets of Prague,
kept as a leper in forced quarantine,

shunned as the pest, avoided like a plague,
he had escaped, mysteriously come
by devious routes, and stolen frontiers, to
the *nalewkas* of Warsaw's sheenydom.

Pressed to reveal his foul identity,
He lied:

One of the anthropophagi was he,
or, if we wished, a denizen of Mars,
the ghost of my father, Conscience — aye,
the spectre of Reason, naked, and with scars;
even became insulting, said he was
Aesop the slave among the animals . . .
Sir Incognito — Rabbi Alias . . .
The eldest elder of Zion . . . said we knew
his numerous varied oriental shapes,
even as we ought to know his present guise —
the man in the jungle, and beset by apes.

It was at this point the S. S. man arrived.
The Jew was interrupted; when he was revived,
He deposed as follows:

At low estate, a beggar, and in flight,
Still do I wear my pride like purple. I
Am undismayed by frenzy or by fright,
And you are those mirrored in my pitying eye.

For you are not the first that I have met —
O I have known them all,
The dwarf dictators, the diminutive dukes,
The heads of straw, the hearts of gall,
Th' imperial plumes of eagles covering rooks!

It is not necessary to name names,
But it may serve anon,
Now to evoke from darkness some dark fames,
Evoke,
Armada'd Spain, that gilded jettison;
And Russia's last descended Romanov,
Descending a dark staircase
To a dank cellar at Ekaterinoslov;
Evoke
The glory that was Babylon that now is gloom;
And Egypt, Egypt, scarcely now recalled
By that lone star that sentries Pharaoh's tomb;
And Carthage, sounded on sand, by water walled;
And Greece — O broken marble! —
And disinterred unresurrected Rome.

These several dominions hunted me;
They all have wished, and more than wished, me dead;
And now, although I do walk raggedly,
I walk, and they are echoes to my tread!

Is it by your devices I shall be undone?

Ah, but you are philosophers, and know
That what has been need not continue so;
The sun has risen: and the sun has set;
Risen again, again descended, yet
To-morrow no bright sun may rise to throw
Rays of inductive reason on Judaeophobic foe.

Is there great turmoil in the sparrow's nest
When that bright bird, the Sun, descends the west?
There is no fear, there is no twittering:
At dawn they will again behold his juvenescent wing!

Such is the very pattern of the world,
Even the sparrows understand;
And in that scheme of things I am enfurled,
Am part thereof, the whole as it was planned,
With increase and abatement rife,
Subject to sorrow, joined to joy —
Earth, its relenting and recurring life!

Yes, but the signet ring, the signet ring!
Since you must know, barbarian, know you shall!
I who now stand before you, a hunted thing,
Pressed and pursued and harried hither and yon,
I was, I am the Emperor Solomon!

O, to and fro upon the face of the earth,
I wandered, crying: Ani Shlomo, but —
But no one believed my birth.

For he now governs in my place and stead,
He who did fling me from Jerusalem
Four hundred parasangs;
Who stole the crown from off my head,
And robed him in my robes, beneath whose hem
The feet of the cock extend, the tail of the demon hangs!
Asmodeus!

Mistake me not: I am no virtuous saint;
Only a man, and like all men, not godly,
Damned by desire —
But I at least waged war, for holy booty,
Against my human taint;
At least sought wisdom, to discern the good;
Whether of men, or birds, or beasts of the wood;
Spread song, spread justice, ever did aspire —
Howbeit, man among men, I failed —
To lay the plan, and work upon the plan
To build the temple of the more-than-man!

But he, the unspeakable prince of malice!
Usurper of my throne, pretender to the Lord's!
Wicked, demoniac, lycanthropous,

Leader of hosts horrific, barbarous hordes,
Master of the worm, pernicious, that cleaves rocks,
The beast that talks,
Asmodeus!—

Who has not heard the plight of his domain?
Learning is banished to the hidden cave;
Wisdom decried, a virtue of the slave;
And justice, both eyes seared, goes tapping with a cane.
His counseler is the wolf. He counsels hate.
His sceptre is a claw.
And love is a high crime against the state.
The fury of the forest
Is the law.

Upon his charnel-throne, in bloodied purple,
Hearkening to that music where the sigh
Pauses to greet the groan, the groan the anguished cry,
Asmodeus sits;
And I —

At this point the S. S. men departed.
The Jew was not revived. He was carried and carted,
and to his present gaoler brought;
awaiting higher pleasure.

                              And further deponent saith not.

RABBI YOM-TOB OF MAYENCE
PETITIONS HIS GOD

I AM no brazen face to hale the Lord
By both His horns of glory into court,
Nor in the talons of the hawk to fix
Subpoenas to assign the heavenly horde;
I am no bailiff at a debtor's door;
I bear no writs against the angels; I
Come not to seize the moveables of the sky.
What the Lord gives, He owes; He owes no more.

Humble I stand before Thy gates,
A beggar in sackcloth, suppliant both palms,
Soliciting Thy alms.
Let them not boot me away, the keepers of Thy gates.
Let them not beat me with Thy lightning rods.
Let them not stone me with Thy thunder-weights.
Humble I stand before Thy gates.

Only in the voice of an earthworm, do I cry:
Descend from Thy tall towers in the sky;
Forsake Thy lonely hermitage; O Lord,
Grant me the Sinai of a single word.
Before Thy feet I spread my prayershawl;
The traces of Thy footsteps I wear out
With kisses; my phylacteries are kin,
Kin to Thy sandal-strings. Grant but Thy grace,

Alight upon these battlements for a space,
And in Thy talk of this and that, make clear,
Before the sun splinters to stars upon the sky,
The how and when, the wherefore and the why . . .

Let there be light
In the two agonies that are my eyes,
And in the dungeon of my heart, a door
Unbarred. Descend, O Lord, and speak.

Then will I say: Let cravens fear
The sword. I know it to be straw.
Let cowards quail before the spear.
To me Death is a toothless jaw.

There is no sign upon the skies,
No witness in the heavens; no
Marvel to which to raise the eyes.
Where the crow flew, there flies the crow.
(He hears not. He is busied. He
Parses the Latin of some monkish homily.)

Not so, oblivious brain, forgetting all.
Blaspheming mouth, not so.
Know what the pious know:

Who hails the cloud for love, must heed
Only the taciturn cloud in speed, —
Who climbs upon the golden stair

Of the sun goes blinded by the glare;
Who counts the stars, will ever find
More stars in the sky than in his mind;
And who addresses him to stone
Upon the high places, is alone.

Not in levin, not in thunder
Shall I behold the sign and wonder,
    But in the still small voice,
    Let me rejoice.
Wherefore Thy will is manifest, O Lord,
Thy will be done.

Be he who yields to baptism, abhorred;
Shunned as a leper be that one.
And unto you, virgins in Israel, be it known
No heathenish paw shall clutch you living. Aye,
Before the starved hound, eager for the bone,
Shall burst the door, lolling a fevered tongue,
Sweet bodies shall smile blithely to the sky.

Blessed this day; this day on which we shall
Make glorious His name. Blessed the sun
Accepting the *Kiddush* of the wine-filled skull.
Blessed this cellar floor, and silent stone,
And benedictions on this hallowed knife
Which pries the door to the eternal life.

BALLAD OF THE THWARTED AXE

(*Coram* the German People's Court)

THE judges sat in their blood-red robes,
The victim in the dock was stood,
The clerk read a number on a writ,
And the room smelled blood.

> *Headsman, headsman, whet your axe,*
> *Against the sparking stone,*
> *The blade that's eaten by the flint,*
> *The better eats the bone!*

The perjurers recite their rote,
The body, manacled, stands mute;
It cannot be they speak of him,
If they do speak the truth.

> *Headsman, headsman, take their words,*
> *Each of a whetstone shape,*
> *And sharpen that good axe of yours,*
> *To meet a stubborn nape!*

The prosecutor weaves his phrase,
With withes of lust, and warpèd lore,
Accused regards his shadow, now
Lying on the floor.

> *Headsman, headsman, that skilled man,*
> *He weaves a beautiful*
> *Red basket, firm and large enough*
> *To hold a severed skull!*

The chief judge in his blood-red robe,
Opens his red-lined book,
And blows therefrom a poisoned breath,
That pales the poor man's look.

> *Headsman, headsman, catch that breath,*
> *That is as sharp as lime!*
> *O, it will eat away the limbs*
> *Of any judge's crime.*

The court is done with its assize
Of overt acts and dead intents;
Now sawdust blots the red ink of
The bleeding documents.

> *Headsman, headsman, — cheated man!*
> *Whom thorough judges mock.*
> *You shall have no use for your axe,*
> *A ghost stands in the dock!*

BALLAD OF THE DAYS OF THE MESSIAH

I

O THE days of the Messiah are at hand, are at hand!
  The days of the Messiah are at hand!
I can hear the air-raid siren, blow away the age of iron,
  Blast away the age of iron
  That was builded on the soft quick-sand.
O the days of the Messiah are at hand!

II

O Leviathan is ready for the feed, for the feed!
  Leviathan is ready for the feed!
And I hold firm to the credo that both powder and torpedo
  Have so fried that good piscedo
He is ready for the eating, scale and seed!
  Leviathan is ready for the feed!

III

Yes, the sacred wine is ready for the good, for the good,
  The wine of yore intended for the good —
Only all that ruddy water has now turned to blood and
    slaughter
  Has fermented into slaughter,
Aged for so long, as it has been, in the wood —
  That wine of yore intended for the good!

IV

O I see him falling! Will he shoot? Will he shoot?
   Will Messiah's falling herald aim and shoot?
'Tis, Elijah, he announces, as he falls from sky, and bounces
   Out of all those silken flounces
Of the heaven-sent and colored parachute:
   Messiah, he is coming, and won't shoot!

V

Don't you hear Messiah coming in his tank, in his tank?
   Messiah in an armor-metalled tank?
I can see the pillared fire, speeding on the metal tire
   Over muck and out of mire
And the seraphim a-shooting from its flank!
   O Messiah, he stands grimy in his tank!

YEHUDA HA-LEVI,
HIS PILGRIMAGE

YEHUDA HA-LEVI, HIS PILGRIMAGE

I

LIVETH the tale, nor ever shall it die!
Upon his scroll the scribe has lettered it.
The learned rabbin, in his homily,
Its telling gilds with verse of holy writ.
O many a darkened Jewerie is lit
By its mere memory. It doth not fail.
Yet, in this latter day, who shall have wit,
Whose cunning of words shall in this day avail
For speech too grieving even for throat of nightingale?

II

Only the fingers of the wind may play
The harp of David on the willow tree;
And Solomon his song, none durst essay.
The sons of Asaph eke have ceased to be;
Dust are their temple throats; and also, he,
The chief musician is now stifled mould.
In Israel is no song save threnodie;
Shall then, for want of singer, stay untold
The tale of the pale princess and the jongleur bold?

III

Bard — and no Levite of degrees, no sweet
Singer in Israel, but a humble wight,

A process-server, a pleader at the leet,
Born, yea, miscarried to a pagan night, —
Sing thou the song that any other might,
Singing for supper; tell the tale as one
Who for a penny sobs his sorry plight,
And let thy words for her be orison
Of saddening evening, and dark midnight, and
    bright dawn.

IV

Whilom in Toledoth, that ancient town,
Founded by Hebrews, built by the conquering Moor,
And governed now by that great Christian Don,
There dwelt the incomparable troubadour —
Bird on the lintel of the ghetto-door!
Brightest of feather of those plumaged throats, —
Melodious ibns of the golden lore,
Who sang the bubbling wine, the riddle's coats,
The ditty, merry or sad, and Love's so difficult notes!

V

Albeit he could joust with the wittiest,
Even with Ezra's sons, their courtesie, —
Apt at the wassail-word, the wedding jest,
The Saracen or Frankish measure, he —
Ermined in *tallith*, crown'd with phylactery,

Halevi, minnesinger of the Lord,
Liege to the manor of divinity,
Has utterly foresworn the profane word.
Homage he gives to God, and carols only at His board.

VI

His was the ballad of the fluttering heart:
The hooded falcon on the wrist of God.
He sang its flights, its venery, its art,
Its moulting, and its final resting sod.
The jewell'd rhyming he devised to laud
The King in whose courts he carolled and was glad,
Were such as never issued from mere clod,
Or from the sage or the divinely mad,
Whether from Mantua or Lesbos or Baghdad.

VII

Did he not also in that wondrous script
Of Al-Kazari chronicle that king,
The heathen begging of the godly-lipped
Some wisdom for his pious hearkening, —
A candle for the dark, — a signet ring
To make the impress of the soul, — that prince
Who covenanted with the mightiest King,
Abjured false testaments and alcorans,
Accepting only Torah and its puissance.

67

VIII

Scorn not the largess lavished on the bard
By Seigneur hearkening the bard's refrain:
The minted moon no merchant ever marr'd;
The sun, the silver currency of Spain;
The mountain flower, the flower of the plain;
And from the beaker of the soul, that wine
Which sours not; and from the bowled brain
Grape clusters torn from paradisal vine;
Honey of Samson's bees; and milk from Pharaoh's kine!

IX

Thus, in that crowded town Castilian,
Where crypted is that psalter, writ on gold
In ink of molten ruby, th' inspired man,
Halevi, served God, luminously-souled.
Aye, and the learned glossators of old
Tell also of his leechcraft, subtil, wise,
For chills and fevers, humors hot and cold,
Simples for all who craved his remedies, —
Nazarite, Moslem, Hebrew — God's ailing entities.

X

Still is there aught which troubles him; it hath
No name nor appellation, yet it is.
Sometimes, it is a shadow on his path,
But thrown by whom he doth not know, y-wis!

Sometimes upon his brow, it is a kiss, —
Was it the wind or feather in the air?
He knoweth not; but there is aught amiss.
Daughter of sound? A footstep on a stair?
And in the synagogue, song heard, and no one there?

XI

The stars are manna in the sky; the moon,
Fleshpot of Egypt. By its light he cons
Old parchment to a Babylonian tune.
He nods, he drowses. Sleep, the Cushite, fawns
Upon Halevi, and he dreams. O once
There were those wizards who could rede these things,
Make clear the dreaming to the dreaming ones —
Baker or cupbearer or young princelings —
But who shall now interpret these imaginings?

XII

Behold in his dream, a castle on a hill,
Moated and massive, ominously-walled!
Of all its towers, one to a pinnacle
Rises, as if by constellations called
To keep all masonry abased, enthralled.
And from that tower is heard a voice, a sigh,
Bitter with Sorrow, sorrow that doth scald
Its hearer as it doth its votary,
At the barred casement of that doleful tower on high.

XIII

O beautiful beyond compare is she,
That lady in the tower of her gaol!
She is the very rose for mystery,
And like the lily is she lily-pale.
She speaketh, and it is as if a tale
Of the sharp thorn were told by the white rose,
Of fragrance that for agony doth fail,
And beauty stabbèd of her dagger'd foes,
Unpetall'd, plundered, and left lying in her throes.

XIV

"I was a princess in my father's hall,
Of all his daughters, his sweet favorite!
Was there a wish, a word my lips let fall, —
The King, my father, not fulfilling it?
O did I wish — as young girls without wit
Might wish — the golden platter of the moon,
Forthwith, I swear, the chamberlain would flit
Hither and yon, send messengers, — 'tis done!
So long ago that was—a dream, remembered, gone!

XV

"Peace in the realm, my father on his throne!
The vintner, swarth, sits drinking underneath
The shadow of his grapes; the hay, new-mown,
Gladdens the peasant on the yellow heath.
And in the garden, I, the King's daughter, wreathe,

Many a flower for the King's delight,
Beauty the late summer doth bequeath, —
Peace in the realm! the generals, old, now fight
Only with bloodless chessmen throughout the
    noiseless night.

XVI

"Suddenly came the foe barbaric, slew,
Plundered and slaughter'd our poor scythe-arm'd youth:
They were a flame that through our hamlets flew
And left not standing palace, nor hut, nor booth.
Utterly without pity, without ruth,
Their sword proclaimed to widow and maid our shame;
The orphan, all affrighted by the uncouth
Stranger, remembered not his own pet name,
Remembering only, as I, the war-cry, flight, and flame.

XVII

"My father! O my father! I know not
Even to this day of his fate. I faint,
I shudder at the dark, the horrible thought.
Perhaps he fled the conqueror's constraint,
A beggar, and unrecognized, a saint,
In some far land of alien wont and word!
It may be — on his shield what blot, what taint! —
He picks the morsels flung beneath the board
By the loud drunken captains feasting with their lord!

XVIII

"And me — alas! — be blotted out that day
  Of ribald jest and ruffianish leer
When the barbarian spied me for his prey!
  Again I see him, and again I hear
His frightening gutturals. Now, in this drear
Tower am I immured, and to be shown
Neighboring princes entertainèd here,
  I am their caged bird, their unwitting clown,
Their most ungracious guest, their tarnished
    trophied crown.

XIX

"Who shall release me from this bondage? What
  Warrior, mounted and plumed, shall some great day
Gallop the highway, jump the noisome moat,
  Dismount, draw sword, and leap his clanging way
Up the long staircase, bloodied with affray,
And at long last, break down this studded door?
It shall not ever be — alack-a-day! —
  Ransom shall not be mine, not ever more,
And perish I shall surely on this stony floor.

XX

"O, if no prince shall ever bring release,
  Nor any soothsayer use wizardry
Encompassing my freedom, then, God please

That soon — or I will surely cease to be —
One little precious gift be granted me!
May I soon hear my good folk speech again!
May I once more, before pale memory
Whitens the mind, hear talk that is like rain
Unto parched fields, like sunshine on the ripening grain!

XXI

"Hast thou some potion that will render me
A bird to flutter from these bars abhorr'd,
Halevi, bring it me; hast thou some plea
To melt the iron of this mailèd horde,
Place it before the Throne; hast thou a sword,
Lift it against my gaolers; at the least,
Bring me thy ringing, winging, singing word."
The shadow lifted, and the dreaming ceased.
The moon had vanished, and the sun smiled from
    the east.

XXII

What fumes within the alembic of his brain
Conjured this dream? What pollen wafted from
Blossoming orchards beyond the turbulent main
Quickens the memory? What mountain drum
Beating beyond the horizon, sends its hum
Echoing softly in Halevi's ear?

In sooth, he knoweth not whence these things come;
But he hath seen a far-off princess, near,
A dark thing happening, and the Lord would make
    it clear!

XXIII

He will no more of herbaries, nor drugs,
Nor physic that is arrogant; he will
Give, as a gift, his phials and his jugs,
And all the script of sage Aristotele.
Begone, Toledo, incense-scented gaol!
He will take staff in hand, and fare him forth
To unknown shores, across the perilous swell
Of seas uncharted, whether south or north;
And he will seek her out, that princess of great worth.

XXIV

Cordova, diadem of Andaluse!
Not from thy robed scholars, splitting hairs,
Nor from thy merchants of bright silk, came news
Of her he sought, nor from the market-fairs
Loud with the gossip of strange pilgrimers.
They had not heard her fame. They knew her not.
Each lifted dinars from his stringed purse
Stamped with some royal head; alas, this wrought
Gold was not precious with the face of her he sought!

XXV

It is a ship, a full white beautiful swan,
Gliding to Africa on the Great Sea!
Alnath, alpherd, alferoz, ald'baran, —
Loveliest blossoms on the heavenly tree
Guiding the slowly-moving argosy.
The mariners sing chanties of sea-folk;
Halevi marvels at the calm blue sea
Whose little waves salaam to the oak,
Breaking the glassy waters. And then the tempest broke!

XXVI

The wind plucked out the stars from heaven; and
The sea, a furious serpent, leaped at the sky,
The ship, a pebble in a tall djinn's hand,
The little men, less than homunculi.
Quoth now the Berber captain, wrathfully:
"There is in our midst an unbelieving cur,
Faring to Egypt with his heathenry!
Into the sea with him, young mariner!
In fish's belly, let him reach Iskandahar!"

XXVII

Answered Halevi: "Pray unto your God!"
"Aye, that we have!" "Then let me pray to mine!"
Then was Halevi's prayer like a rod

Smiting the wild uplifted wave supine.
To liturgy heart-rending came divine
Answer unto the sea-swept wind-swept **dove!**
The mariners gape now at the calm brine
And now stare at the kindly sky above
Where ald'baran, alnath, alpherd, alferoz **rove!**

XXVIII

Are they not written in the annal **books**
The places of his perilous journeying:
The bright saharas, shimmering, with **no brooks;**
The deserts wild; the mountains harboring
Assassins; and the sweet oases spring
Where tribes fanatic curl in the scimitar?
And is not, too, recorded the welcoming
That **Cairo,** Demieyet, Iskandahar,
Made for the learned minstrel coming **from afar?**

XXIX

But nowhere did he find the face he sought.
The silent pyramids, the ancient Nile
Knowing so many secrets, knew her not.
Shereef and scarrèd cid and rabbin smile
At this his search, and bid him tarry awhile
In new Mizraim where no pharaoh is;
In vain: the shadow grows upon the dial;
Time flies; and in the dungeon of distress
Waits, pale, her hair hung loose, the **beautiful princess.**

XXX

What Asian cities did his sandals shun?
He sought them all; the cities of great bazars;
The Gates where justice triumphs in the sun,
The village of the clanging armourers.
He sought them all; there where the gardener mars
The rose to attar, and the too-sweet air
Silences birds, and makes to swoon the stars!
He was to the fief of the crippled conjuror.
Ever he chased a shadow in a vision of nowhere.

XXXI

Weary, and footsore, and in spirit low,
At length, at long last, after many days,
He is upon the dusty roads that go
Bowing to Palestine. O offer praise
Halevi, to thy Lord, for thine eyes gaze
Now upon land that is that holy stem
Whose flower, in heaven, blossoms forth ablaze
A flower, a flame, a talismanic gem —
Lift up thine eyes — the glorious Hierusalem!

XXXII

O wondrous miracle that came to pass!
The blindfold of the dream is dropped away.
It is no vision, seen as through a glass, —
It is the brightness of the high noon-day.

77

Behold the princess in her sad array!
Certes 'tis she, and no vain stratagem!
It is she whom the vision did soothsay!
The princess of the fallen diadem!
Jerusalem, the princess! Fair Jerusalem!

XXXIII

Aye, but that dark dreaming is now bright.
The princess Zion is that princess fair
Gaoled by the cross-marked arrogant Frankish knight!
Still is she beautiful, though full of care;
Still is the jasmine fragrant from her hair
And still within her eyes is, shining, kept
Remembered sunshine. But despair, despair
Like a hot wind of the desert, overswept
Halevi, and he sang what was not song. He wept.

XXXIV

"Grieving for them, thy captive sons who are
The last sheep of thy flock, O Zion, take,
Accept from them their greeting from afar,
Their greeting and their longing and their ache.
Receive the homage of thy vassal, whose
Tears, like the dew of Hermon, seek thy hills,
Where he would be a jackal, all night long
        Wailing thy bitter news,
Where he would dream away thy manacles,
And be the harp melodious for thy song!

XXXV

"Peniel! Bethel! Mahanayim! sod
Where walked thy saints, where rests the Immanence,
Whose gates are open to the gates of God,
Whose light is not the light of firmaments
But the illumination of the Lord!
Shrines holy! Where I would pour out my soul
As was the spirit of the sacred One
     Upon you once out-poured,
How have you fallen to an evil dole,
Where slaves now lord it from your sullied throne!

XXXVI

"Thy ruins, thy waste places, and thy void,
Thy dwellings rendered rubble and small rock,
The chambers of thy cherubim destroyed —
Yea, there though bleeding, barefoot, would I walk.
I will cut off my hair, and that day curse
That flung thy crowned ones among heathen foes;
I'll fast, for food and drink must surely reek
     When I behold the curs,
Tearing the lion's litter, and day shows
The eagle bleeding from the raven's beak!

XXXVII

"O Zion, altogether beautiful!
Thy sons rejoice them in thy time of peace,
And in thy sorrow, their cup, too, is full.

They weep thy ruins, yet they never cease
From striving towards thee from captivity,
They bend the knee unto thy gates, thy sons,
Scattered on mountains, driven over seas,
　　Remembering Zion, thee,
Yearning to touch the plinth of thy shattered stones
O but to touch the boughs of thy palm-trees!

XXXVIII

"Can Shinar and Pathros equal thee for glory?
Can Urim and Thummim be surpassed by spells?
With whom compare thy kings, thy prophets hoary,
Thy Levites and thy singers? All things else
Will pass away — idol, idolater —
Only thy crown is for eternity!
Thou art God's dwelling place, His goodly booth!
　　O none is happier
Than he who with thee waits thy dawn to see
Thee once again as Thou wast in thy youth!

XXXIX

"God granted that I might go wandering
Where He to seer and prophet was revealed.
God gave me wings that I might fly; and fling
My broken heart upon thy broken field.
O, I will fall upon my face, and kiss
Thy very stones, so blessed in thine earth;

I will take hold of thee, thy clods, thy soil,
    Thy very dustiness,
And hold it as a thing of extreme worth —
Prized above rubies, and the richest spoil."

XL

Would that with these his tears this tale might end,
Even with this sad guerdon, this poor meed!
Zion abased by the irreverend,
Yet Zion, seen; Zion beheld, in deed!
But so 'twas not ordained, not so decreed;
Lo, from afar, and shouting a wild oath
Rideth an Arab on his thundering steed.
Nameless that rider, save for war-name, Death.
Zion, O Princess, receive thy minstrel's trampled breath!

XLI

Murdered, the minnesinger of the Lord!
Where rest his bones? None knows. Surely he dwells
In the third temple of the hallowed word,
Where Zion, even now, still hears the bells
Of high-priest moving at his rituals,
Where the fair princess still hears prophecy,
And joyful music, and the oracles
Consolatory of her misery,
Saying: The daugher of the king will yet be free.

XLII

Liveth the tale, nor ever shall it die!
The princess in her tower grows not old.
For that she heard his charmed minstrelsy,
She is forever young. Her crown of gold,
Bartered and customed, auctioned, hawked and sold,
Is still for no head but her lovely head.
What if the couch be hard, the cell be cold,
The warder's keys unrusted, stale the bread?
Halevi sang her song, and she is comforted!